"Simple and straightforward, Meet Me in the Bible is a wc
foundational skills in studying the Bible. If you want to ː
Scripture for God's truths and applying it to your life, this is an incredible guide."

Laura Wifler, Cofounder, Risen Motherhood; coauthor, *Risen Motherhood:
Gospel Hope for Everyday Moments*

"I was greeted by the bright smile of Colleen Searcy over thirty years ago when
I walked into a youth group in West Texas as a freckle-faced, curly headed, unbe-
lieving teenager. Over the last three decades, I have watched Colleen cling to God's
word, teach God's word, sing God's word, and live God's word. If you are looking to
meet God in the Scriptures, I can think of no better guide than my friend Colleen.
She will help you taste and see that the Lord is good!"

Shane Barnard, singer-songwriter, Shane and Shane

"Colleen Searcy is one of my favorite Bible teachers. You will sense her open-armed
ministry within the framework of her Meet Me in the Bible series, in which she's
thoughtfully prepared a table for women to feast on God's word. Whether you are
an individual hungry to know God more, a small group desiring an accessible way
to study together, or a women's ministry leader looking for a foundational resource
for your teaching team, the Meet Me in the Bible series is a trustworthy guide."

Caroline Saunders, author, *Come Home: Tracing God's Promise of Home
through Scripture*

"I've benefited from Colleen's wisdom, teaching, and partnership in ministry for a
number of years. She is a gifted Bible teacher who uses her skills to invite others
into biblical literacy. In the Meet Me in the Bible series, she provides what few
studies do—an opportunity for women to gather for both in-person teaching and
discussion. You will be equipped to not only study for yourself but also cultivate
teaching gifts in the lives of the women in your church. I can't wait to recommend
this to my ministry friends."

Courtney Reissig, author, *Teach Me to Feel: Worshiping through the Psalms
in Every Season of Life*

"As the CEO of a worldwide mission agency, I highly recommend Colleen Searcy's Meet Me in the Bible series for anyone interested in going deeper in their study of the Bible. Colleen uses a structured approach with guiding prompts that are fully interactive and enhance your reflection on Scripture. These books are helpful resources for pursuing individual study or leading a Bible study group, and these studies are culturally relevant for all groups of people. Meet Me in the Bible is an excellent and well-rounded framework that can make studying the Bible a more engaging and enriching experience for anyone."

Kurt Nelson, CEO, East-West Ministries

"I have seen firsthand the fruit of Meet Me in the Bible. Colleen's accessible framework for studying the Scripture has had a large and lasting impact on our church. Many in our congregation are still reaping the benefits of her investment in our women's ministry. If you are a seasoned student of the Scripture or are just getting started, Meet Me in the Bible will launch you into a greater exploration of the Bible and a deeper enjoyment of the God it reveals."

JR Vassar, Lead Pastor, Church at the Cross, Grapevine, Texas; author, *Glory Hunger*

THE STORY OF
ABRAHAM

Meet Me in the Bible Studies

Colossians and Philemon

The Story of Abraham

MEET ME IN THE BIBLE

THE STORY OF ABRAHAM

AN 8-WEEK BIBLE STUDY

COLLEEN D. SEARCY

Foreword by Jen Wilkin

CROSSWAY®

WHEATON, ILLINOIS

The Story of Abraham: An 8-Week Bible Study

© 2025 by Colleen D. Searcy

Published by Crossway
        1300 Crescent Street
        Wheaton, Illinois 60187

Tool 1, "Bible Timeline," designed by Brooke Hawkins.

Definitions in Tool 4, "The Attributes of God," are taken from or informed by *The ABCs of God* by Jill Nelson. © 1998, 2016 Jill Nelson. Illustrations Truth78.org. All rights reserved. Used by permission.

Cover illustration and design by Brooke Hawkins

First printing 2025

Printed in China

Trade paperback ISBN: 978-1-4335-9687-2
ePub ISBN: 978-1-4335-9689-6
PDF ISBN: 978-1-4335-9688-9

Crossway is a publishing ministry of Good News Publishers.

RRD			34	33	32	31	30	29	28	27	26	25
15	14	13	12	11	10	9	8	7	6	5	4	3	2	1

CONTENTS

FOREWORD

For the past twenty-five years, my primary place of ministry has been the local church, and my primary aim has been to build Bible literacy among women. So, naturally, any time I'm asked to endorse a resource, I ask myself how it will serve that context. That's why I'm particularly excited to bring to your attention the Meet Me in the Bible series.

When evaluating a resource, I hold two important questions in view: (1) Is this from a trustworthy voice? and (2) Does this challenge those who use it to grow in their ability to read and understand the Scriptures? I want to help answer both of those questions for you as you consider how the Meet Me in the Bible series might help you personally, or those you serve in your church.

In terms of the trustworthiness of the author, I can speak with confidence that Colleen Searcy is an excellent guide. I first met Colleen in 2008, about a year after moving to Dallas and joining a new church. I was looking for other women in the church who shared my desire to see women equipped with solid discipleship opportunities. Colleen and I went to coffee, and I knew I had found a like-minded partner. Since that time, we have together taught, written curriculum, led teams, and prayed—all from that desire to see God's daughters grounded in the Scriptures. Colleen is not only theologically and biblically solid; she is a gifted teacher, humble and kind, and a faithful friend.

In terms of the usefulness of the resource, Meet Me in the Bible so closely aligns with my own philosophy of teaching that I can recommend it eagerly. It's a brilliant combination of a Scripture journal and a guide for growing in Bible literacy. It encourages the user to practice the time-tested method of "observe, interpret, apply" in a way that allows understanding to grow gradually. It presses us to be active learners rather than passive consumers, not rushing to commentaries, but sitting with the text, patiently waiting for our own understanding to begin to emerge. For those who know my method and Bible studies, Meet Me in the Bible will feel familiar in the best ways.

It is a streamlined approach suitable for personal study as well as an excellent foundation for group discussion and teaching environments.

The skills taught in each Meet Me in the Bible study will help you understand a particular book of the Bible better. But they will also help you understand *any* book of the Bible better as you grow in your ability to use those skills. And because application focuses on relationship—with God, self, and others—these skills will help you to live and love like a Christ follower.

So it is my pleasure to commend to you both a trusted guide and a trustworthy resource. My guess is that if you had come to coffee with Colleen and me on that day some years ago, you would have shared our excitement to see women growing in their love of the Scriptures and of the God they proclaim. What we want for you is to be able to serve your local church, whether in a classroom or a living room, with good tools and the confidence to use them. My prayer is that you would take what Colleen has created and combine it with an invitation to the women God has placed in your sphere of influence—a simple invitation: Meet me in the Bible! No sweeter fellowship is found than in that meeting place. May your time spent there yield the richest of treasures.

JEN WILKIN
Bible teacher; author, *Women of the Word*;
None Like Him; and *In His Image*

MEET ME IN THE BIBLE
A Simple Framework for Reading the Bible and Enjoying God

God delights in revealing himself, and one of the primary ways he reveals himself is through the Bible. My deep desire is for people to know and enjoy God through the study of his word. I want people with all kinds of personalities and learning styles to grow in confidence that they can read and study their Bibles. This framework of Bible study was designed to provide helpful structure and a lot of freedom for the studier.

The *Why* behind Meet Me in the Bible

Meet Me in the Bible is a simple, five-step framework designed to help you read your Bible. It is not a fill-in-the-blank study. After numerous conversations with women over many years of ministry, I've found that countless women do Bible studies, yet few feel confident opening the Bible and reading it on their own. And although many women desire to lead a Bible study, few feel equipped to do so. Meet Me in the Bible offers a method to help you do both.

How to Use Meet Me in the Bible

This framework was designed for either individual or group Bible study, and it incorporates the time-tested stages of Bible reading: observation, interpretation, and application. Prompts are provided on your bookmark to help you observe, interpret, and apply the Scriptures. You will also be prompted to use simple and accessible tools as you study. You will grow in confidence and find your pace as you practice observing, interpreting, and applying the Scriptures again and again. You can use this framework to study any book of the Bible.

For Group Study

If you are doing this study as part of a group, you will want to complete each lesson before you meet. Each lesson is divided into five doable steps rather than five assigned days, to allow flexibility. You can work through one step each day or the whole lesson in one sitting. Find the pace that works best for you. No matter how much of the lesson you are able to complete, please don't skip gathering with your Bible study group. You will benefit from your group, and your group will be encouraged by your presence.

Meet Me in the Bible studies are meant to be flexible. Group studies can opt to meet in small groups for discussion and a time of teaching or simply meet for discussion only.

TIPS FOR GROUPS THAT OPT TO MEET FOR BOTH A TIME OF DISCUSSION AND A TIME OF TEACHING

- If this is your group's first Meet Me in the Bible study, be sure each participant is familiar with how to use the Meet Me in the Bible framework before you meet. You can find my video on how to use the Meet Me in the Bible framework at colleensearcy.com/mmibteaching. In this video, I demonstrate how to cross-reference, quickly check other translations, and more, using simple and free digital tools.

- For the first meeting, teachers will want to cover the Getting Started section before discussion. One of the greatest Bible study tools available is the historical context of the Bible book you are studying. To have the best chance of interpreting the Scriptures correctly, you need to know who the author was, whom he was writing to, the literary style he used, and what was happening in the world when he wrote it. I cover the answers to these questions in my "Getting Started" video, which you will find at colleensearcy.com/mmibteaching.

- After answering those preliminary questions, move to small-group discussion. Spend some time getting to know one another by asking questions like, What brought you to this study? Why are you excited to study this content? What piqued your curiosity from the Getting Started questions?

- For all future meetings, you can gather for discussion before or after the teaching. I suggest that you gather *before* the teaching. You will be amazed at the insights gained as each participant shares what was discovered during personal study. Confidence will grow as you learn from one another's discoveries. Tips for discussion:

- The prompts on your bookmark make good points of discussion. (What did you learn from the repeated words? What was hard to understand? What did you learn about people?)

- Content-specific discussion questions for each lesson can be found in Tool 7 of the Tool Kit.

- Additional historical context is given in the questions in Tool 7 of the Tool Kit.

- The bounce questions in Tool 7 of the Tool Kit are intended to jumpstart discussion and provide an easy transition to the content.

- Discussion leaders may use as many or as few discussion questions from Tool 7 as they'd like. These questions were written to help you think deeply about the text. Many of the questions do not have one right answer and are meant to encourage further thought and robust discussion. Questions with one correct answer (e.g., What did Paul say about sin in verse 12?) can feel like a quiz rather than an invitation into conversation.

- Discussion leaders *do* want to plan which questions they will cover and think through their own answers before the group meets. They *do not* need to feel pressure to answer every question that surfaces during Bible study. The purpose of Bible study is not to impress with our knowledge; it is to grow in our knowledge of and love for God as we get to know him better through the study of his word. Enjoy being a colearner with those you are studying alongside. If the questions that surface are not answered in the teaching time, you can circle back with your group after you've had time to think further about them.

- Use the prayer pages in Tool 6 of the Tool Kit to record personal prayer requests and the prayers of those you are studying alongside.

TIPS FOR GROUPS THAT OPT TO MEET FOR DISCUSSION ONLY

- If this is your group's first Meet Me in the Bible study, be sure each participant watches my video on how to use the Meet Me in the Bible framework before you meet. You can find it at colleensearcy.com /mmibteaching. In this video, I demonstrate how to cross-reference, quickly check other translations, and more, using simple and free digital tools.

- For the first meeting, be prepared to discuss the Getting Started section. One of the greatest Bible study tools available is the historical context of the Bible book you are studying. To have the best chance of interpreting the Scriptures correctly, you need to know who the author was, whom he was writing to, the literary style he used, and what was happening in the world when he wrote it. I answer these questions in my "Getting Started" video at colleensearcy.com/mmibteaching.

- Spend some time getting to know one another by asking questions like, What brought you to this study? Why are you excited to study this content? What piqued your curiosity from the Getting Started questions?

- For all future meetings:

  - The prompts on your bookmark make good points of discussion: What did you learn from the repeated words? What was hard to understand? What did you learn about people?

  - Content-specific discussion questions for each lesson can be found in Tool 7 of the Tool Kit.

  - The bounce questions in Tool 7 of the Tool Kit are intended to jumpstart discussion and provide an easy transition to the content.

- Additional historical context is given in the questions found in Tool 7 of the Tool Kit.

- Discussion leaders may use as many or as few discussion questions from Tool 7 as they'd like. These questions were written to help you think deeply about the text. Many of the questions do not have one right answer and are meant to encourage further thought and robust discussion. Questions with one correct answer (e.g., What did Paul say about sin in verse 12?) can feel like a quiz rather than an invitation into conversation.

- Discussion leaders *do* want to plan on which questions they will cover and think through their own answers before the group meets. They *do not* need to feel pressure to answer every question that surfaces during Bible study. The purpose of Bible study is not to impress with our knowledge; it is to grow in our knowledge of and love for God as we get to know him better through the study of his word. When stumped by a question, you can say something like, "That is a great question! I'd like to give that more thought and circle back next time we meet." Then have fun studying! Enjoy being a colearner with those you are studying alongside. Ask God to help you with the questions that surface. He is delighted to meet you in the Bible. What a great discussion you will have the next time you meet!

- Use the prayer pages in Tool 6 of the Tool Kit to record personal prayer requests and the prayers of those you are studying alongside.

For Individual Study

- If you are doing this study on your own, you will want to begin by watching my video on how to use the Meet Me in the Bible framework. You can find it at colleensearcy.com/mmibteaching. In this video, I demonstrate how to cross-reference, quickly check other translations, and more, using simple and free digital tools.

- Be sure to complete the Getting Started section before diving in to study the passages of Scripture. One of the greatest Bible study tools available is the historical context of the Bible book you are studying. When you study a passage that is hard to understand, overlay the passage with the context. To have the best chance of interpreting the Scriptures correctly, we need to know who the author was, whom he was writing to, the literary style he used, and what was happening in the world when he wrote it. I answer these questions in my "Getting Started" video at colleensearcy.com/mmibteaching.

- After completing the Getting Started section, each lesson is divided into five doable steps rather than five assigned days, to allow flexibility. You can work through one step each day or work through the whole lesson in one sitting. Find the pace that works best for you.

- For a deeper dive, use the questions in Tool 7 of the Tool Kit. Additional historical context is also given within the questions. These questions were written to help you think deeply about the text.

- Use the prayer pages in Tool 6 of the Tool Kit to record your prayers while you study.

What's Included in This Study

Bible Study Bookmark

All Meet Me in the Bible studies include a bookmark with the time-tested stages of Bible reading (Observe, Interpret, and Apply) on the front. You will see the five-step framework for reading the Bible on the back of the bookmark, including prompts to help you observe, interpret, and apply the Scriptures. You will also be prompted to pause in your study to listen to and enjoy God. He wants to meet you in your study of the Bible! Although the Bible study bookmark and the Bible study book were designed to work together, your bookmark can also be used alone. It was designed to help you study any book of the Bible, and my hope is that you will use your bookmark again and again.

Bible Study Book

The book includes word-for-word Bible text. Mark it up! If you love highlighters, highlight away! If you prefer to draw symbols, grab colored pencils and go for it. Or simply underline with your favorite pen. Your Bible study book also includes titles and designated spaces that correspond with the titles and prompts on your bookmark. Additionally, you will find blank note pages throughout your book to use as you wish. Draw a chart, sketch an image, or write the lyrics to a song. Each lesson concludes with an important wrap-up question to prompt you to consider what you discovered in the Scriptures.

Meet Me in the Bible Tool Kit

Tool 1: *Bible Timeline.* Place an *X* on the simple timeline of the Bible to indicate where the scriptures you are studying land in the whole story of the Bible.

Tool 2: *Map.* Referencing a map while studying is a helpful reminder that these are stories of real people in real places.

Tool 3: *Bible Genres.* Knowing the literary style of the book of the Bible you are studying is key to correct interpretation. Just as you would approach the poems of Wordsworth differently than you would approach a history book about World War II, there are nuances to different literary styles in the Bible that must be kept in mind while interpreting and applying the Scriptures. Use this resource to identify the literary style of the book you are studying.

Tool 4: *Attributes of God.* You will be prompted to use this tool each week. You may want to mark it with a paper clip so you can turn there easily. The ultimate goal of Bible study is to know and love God, and my prayer is that your hope will be further anchored in him as you are reminded of his attributes.

Tool 5: *Bookmark Content.* All the information on your bookmark is included here for your convenience.

Tool 6: *Prayer Pages.* Use these pages to record personal prayers and prayer requests of those studying alongside you.

Tool 7: *Questions for Further Thought and Discussion.* Use as many or as few of these questions as you'd like in your individual or group study. Additional historical context is included in the questions. The bounce questions are intended to jumpstart discussion and provide an easy transition to the content. The remaining questions were written to help you think deeply about the text.

Additional Tools for Your Study

1. *Different Bible translations.* Reading Scripture verses in different Bible translations can give helpful insight as you study. This book includes the ESV translation. Other translations I recommend are the New International Version (NIV), the New Living Translation (NLT), the Christian Standard Bible (CSB), and the New American Standard Bible (NASB). I use The Message as a commentary when I study.

2. *Dictionary and thesaurus.* Look up unfamiliar words as well as "church" words such as *atonement*, *propitiation*, and *covenant*. You will be surprised how much clarity can be gained by reading simple definitions and synonyms in a dictionary or thesaurus.[1]

3. *Cross-references.* Cross-references are included in study Bibles, usually in the middle or at the bottom of a page. A cross-reference is a marker in the Bible pointing to other passages of Scripture with related words and themes. It is usually designated with a superscript (tiny, raised) letter. Cross-referencing is a way to use Scripture to rightly interpret Scripture. You can also use digital tools to cross-reference.[2]

4. *Study Bible footnotes.* If you have a study Bible, the provided footnotes give helpful insights.[3] Wait to check footnotes until after you've observed the text and attempted interpretation using other translations, a dictionary, and cross-references. Resist the temptation to jump to someone else's thoughts before observing and interpreting on your own. Enjoy being curious and see what you discover!

5. *Commentaries.* Commentaries can be helpful in Bible study, but wait to use commentaries until after you've observed the text and attempted interpretation using other translations, a dictionary, and cross-references. Ask God for insight as you study, and be willing to wait to hear from him. Again, resist the temptation to jump to someone else's thoughts before observing and interpreting on your own. For help choosing commentaries, begin by asking trusted leaders about their favorites.[4]

The ultimate goal of Bible study is to know and love God. So observe, interpret, apply, and enjoy God! Stay in conversation with him, asking him to help you understand the Scriptures. Ask him your hard questions. Listen to him. He wants to meet you in your study of the Bible!

WHY STUDY THE STORY OF ABRAHAM?

Twelve chapters of the Bible are dedicated to the story of Abraham and his family. And Abraham is mentioned more than seventy times in the New Testament. He is certainly a key figure in the history of the Christian faith. His story helps us understand the rest of the Bible.

The account of Abraham and his family is found in the book of Genesis. Genesis is the book of beginnings—the beginning of the world, the beginning of people, the beginning of family, the beginning of sin, the beginning of languages—and in this book of beginnings, we see the plan for redemption begin to unfold. Genesis also includes the record of the beginning of the Hebrew people, the people through whom God will show all other people groups what he is like. God begins the Hebrew people with Abram and Sarai (later called Abraham and Sarah), a childless couple from Ur.

Throughout the rest of the Bible, we see their story broaden to include all those who place their faith in Jesus Christ (Rom. 4:11–12). If you have placed your faith in Jesus Christ, the story of Abraham is the story of your family. You will find your ancestors, Abraham and Sarah, to be very relatable.

Both will fail. And both will demonstrate great faith.

Both will shoulder great heartache. And both will experience miracles from God.

Both will feel forgotten by God. And both will be reminded that he always does what he says he will do.

Both are called to a life of faith, believing the impossible.

Both will give rise to the chosen people of God, their descendants outnumbering the stars. One of those descendants will be Jesus Christ, the bright morning star.

Enjoy getting to know God better and better as you study the story of Abraham.

Joyfully,
COLLEEN SEARCY

GETTING STARTED IN THE STORY OF ABRAHAM

We have our best chance of understanding the story of Abraham if we overlay the text in Genesis with important context. Below are context questions to address before you begin the study.[5]

1. Who wrote the story of Abraham, recorded in the book of Genesis?

....

....

....

....

2. When was the book of Genesis written?

....

....

....

....

3. To whom was it written and for what purpose?

....

....

....

....

4. In what style was the book of Genesis written? Turn to Tool 3 in the Tool Kit for help identifying the genre.[6]

5. What are the central themes of the book of Genesis?

6. Turn to Tool 1 in the Tool Kit. Place an *X* on the timeline to determine where the story of Abraham lands in the whole story of the Bible.

1

THE CALL OF ABRAM AND
THE JOURNEY TO EGYPT

Genesis 11:27–13:1

THE CALL OF ABRAM AND
THE JOURNEY TO EGYPT
Genesis 11:27–13:1

²⁷ Now these are the generations of Terah. Terah fathered Abram, Nahor, and Haran; and Haran fathered Lot. ²⁸ Haran died in the presence of his father Terah in the land of his kindred, in Ur of the Chaldeans. ²⁹ And Abram and Nahor took wives. The name of Abram's wife was Sarai, and the name of Nahor's wife, Milcah, the daughter of Haran the father of Milcah and Iscah. ³⁰ Now Sarai was barren; she had no child.

³¹ Terah took Abram his son and Lot the son of Haran, his grandson, and Sarai his daughter-in-law, his son Abram's wife, and they went forth together from Ur of the Chaldeans to go into the land of Canaan, but when they came to Haran, they settled there. ³² The days of Terah were 205 years, and Terah died in Haran.

^{12:1} Now the LORD said to Abram, "Go from your country and your kindred and your father's house to the land that I will show you. ² And I will make of you a great nation, and I will bless you and make your name great, so that you will be a blessing. ³ I will bless those who bless you, and him who dishonors you I will curse, and in you all the families of the earth shall be blessed."

⁴ So Abram went, as the LORD had told him, and Lot went with him. Abram was seventy-five years old when he departed from Haran. ⁵ And Abram took Sarai his wife, and Lot his brother's son, and all their possessions that they had gathered, and the people that they had acquired in Haran, and they set out to go to the land of Canaan. When they came to the land of Canaan, ⁶ Abram passed through the land to the place at Shechem, to the oak of Moreh. At that time the Canaanites were in the land. ⁷ Then the LORD appeared to Abram and said, "To your offspring I will give this land." So he built there an altar to the LORD, who had appeared to him. ⁸ From there he moved to the

hill country on the east of Bethel and pitched his tent, with Bethel on the west and Ai on the east. And there he built an altar to the LORD and called upon the name of the LORD. ⁹ And Abram journeyed on, still going toward the Negeb.

¹⁰ Now there was a famine in the land. So Abram went down to Egypt to sojourn there, for the famine was severe in the land. ¹¹ When he was about to enter Egypt, he said to Sarai his wife, "I know that you are a woman beautiful in appearance, ¹² and when the Egyptians see you, they will say, 'This is his wife.' Then they will kill me, but they will let you live. ¹³ Say you are my sister, that it may go well with me because of you, and that my life may be spared for your sake." ¹⁴ When Abram entered Egypt, the Egyptians saw that the woman was very beautiful. ¹⁵ And when the princes of Pharaoh saw her, they praised her to Pharaoh. And the woman was taken into Pharaoh's house. ¹⁶ And for her sake he dealt well with Abram; and he had sheep, oxen, male donkeys, male servants, female servants, female donkeys, and camels.

¹⁷ But the LORD afflicted Pharaoh and his house with great plagues because of Sarai, Abram's wife. ¹⁸ So Pharaoh called Abram and said, "What is this you have done to me? Why did you not tell me that she was your wife? ¹⁹ Why did you say, 'She is my sister,' so that I took her for my wife? Now then, here is your wife; take her, and go." ²⁰ And Pharaoh gave men orders concerning him, and they sent him away with his wife and all that he had.

¹³:¹ So Abram went up from Egypt, he and his wife and all that he had, and Lot with him, into the Negeb.

NOTES

OBSERVE: WHAT DOES THE PASSAGE SAY?

Step 1: Setting and Summary

Key Characters and Locations

CHARACTERS:

- *Abram.* Son of Terah, husband of Sarai. He heard from God and obeyed.
- *Sarai.* Wife of Abram. The author is clear that she was barren.
- *The Lord.* Spoke to Abram and promised him land, blessing, a great name, and many descendants.
- *Pharaoh.* Ruler of Egypt.

LOCATIONS:

- *Ur.* Abram and Sarai's homeland before the Lord called them to go.
- *Haran.* Abram's family stopped here rather than traveling all the way to Canaan.
- *Canaan.* Abram's destination. The land God gave to Abram's offspring.
- *The Negeb.* The region between Canaan and Egypt, south of the region that will eventually become Judah.
- *Egypt.* Where Abram sojourned when famine struck Canaan.

Summary of the Passage

What Stood Out to You or Piqued Your Curiosity?

Step 2: Key Words and Phrases

Remember to look at the prompts on your Bible study bookmark as you observe the text.

- "I will" (6 times!)
- bless/blessing (5 times). Dictionary definition: "to invoke divine care for."[7]

Remember to enjoy God and listen as you study. Move to a time of prayer after you observe, recording your prayer on the prayer pages in Tool 6 of the Tool Kit.

NOTES

INTERPRET: WHAT DOES THE PASSAGE MEAN?

Step 3: What Was Hard to Understand?

Questions

- *Why did Abram's family settle in Haran? Why didn't they go all the way to Canaan instead?*
- *Why was Pharaoh afflicted when Abram sinned? And why did Abram get to leave Egypt as a wealthy man? It seems like Abram is rewarded for his sin.*

Insights from Cross-References, Other Translations, and/or the Context

Remember that historical context is one of the greatest Bible study tools available. Keep asking the questions: Who wrote this? When did he write it? Where does this land in the whole story of the Bible? How would these words land on the ears of the original hearers?

- *Why did Abram's family settle in Haran?* Why didn't they go all the way to Canaan instead? In a cross-reference, Acts 7:2–4, we read that after Abram's father died, God removed him (NIV has "sent him") from Haran to Canaan. It sounds like the stop in Haran had something to do with Abram's father, Terah. We don't know for sure why Abram stopped in Haran, but we know that God did not let him stay there.
- *Why was Pharaoh afflicted when Abram sinned? And why did Abram get to leave Egypt as a wealthy man? It seems like Abram is rewarded for his sin.* Hint: Look back at the context on page 13 to gain insight. Who wrote the book of Genesis? To whom was he writing? Where had they just come from? How might the story of Abram being ordered to leave by Pharaoh, then leaving Egypt with riches, encourage them?

Remember to turn to the Questions for Further Thought and Discussion in Tool 7 for a deeper dive. Additional historical context is also given within the questions.

Step 4: What Did You Learn about God?

Refer to the attributes of God in Tool 4 if needed.

Remember to enjoy God and listen as you study. Move to a time of prayer after you interpret, recording your prayer on the prayer pages in Tool 6.

NOTES

APPLY: HOW WILL YOU APPLY THE PASSAGE?

Step 5: What Did You Learn about People?

Others

Remember to look at the prompts on your Bible study bookmark as you apply the text.

Yourself

- *Is there a command to obey? An example to follow? A sin to confess? A warning to heed? An encouragement to receive?*
- *What action step will you take?*

Wrap Up: What Did You Discover in the Scriptures That Was Important to You?

Remember to enjoy God and listen as you study. Move to a time of prayer after you apply, recording your prayer on the prayer pages in Tool 6.

2

ABRAM, LOT, AND MELCHIZEDEK

Genesis 13:2–14:24

ABRAM, LOT, AND MELCHIZEDEK
Genesis 13:2–14:24

²Now Abram was very rich in livestock, in silver, and in gold. ³And he journeyed on from the Negeb as far as Bethel to the place where his tent had been at the beginning, between Bethel and Ai, ⁴to the place where he had made an altar at the first. And there Abram called upon the name of the LORD. ⁵And Lot, who went with Abram, also had flocks and herds and tents, ⁶so that the land could not support both of them dwelling together; for their possessions were so great that they could not dwell together, ⁷and there was strife between the herdsmen of Abram's livestock and the herdsmen of Lot's livestock. At that time the Canaanites and the Perizzites were dwelling in the land.

⁸Then Abram said to Lot, "Let there be no strife between you and me, and between your herdsmen and my herdsmen, for we are kinsmen. ⁹Is not the whole land before you? Separate yourself from me. If you take the left hand, then I will go to the right, or if you take the right hand, then I will go to the left." ¹⁰And Lot lifted up his eyes and saw that the Jordan Valley was well watered everywhere like the garden of the LORD, like the land of Egypt, in the direction of Zoar. (This was before the LORD destroyed Sodom and Gomorrah.) ¹¹So Lot chose for himself all the Jordan Valley, and Lot journeyed east. Thus they separated from each other. ¹²Abram settled in the land of Canaan, while Lot settled among the cities of the valley and moved his tent as far as Sodom. ¹³Now the men of Sodom were wicked, great sinners against the LORD.

¹⁴The LORD said to Abram, after Lot had separated from him, "Lift up your eyes and look from the place where you are, northward and southward and eastward and westward, ¹⁵for all the land that you see I will give to you and to your offspring forever. ¹⁶I will make your offspring as the dust of the earth, so that if one can count the dust of the earth, your offspring also can be counted. ¹⁷Arise, walk through the length and the breadth of the land, for

I will give it to you." ¹⁸ So Abram moved his tent and came and settled by the oaks of Mamre, which are at Hebron, and there he built an altar to the LORD.

¹⁴:¹ In the days of Amraphel king of Shinar, Arioch king of Ellasar, Chedorlaomer king of Elam, and Tidal king of Goiim, ² these kings made war with Bera king of Sodom, Birsha king of Gomorrah, Shinab king of Admah, Shemeber king of Zeboiim, and the king of Bela (that is, Zoar). ³ And all these joined forces in the Valley of Siddim (that is, the Salt Sea). ⁴ Twelve years they had served Chedorlaomer, but in the thirteenth year they rebelled. ⁵ In the fourteenth year Chedorlaomer and the kings who were with him came and defeated the Rephaim in Ashteroth-karnaim, the Zuzim in Ham, the Emim in Shaveh-kiriathaim, ⁶ and the Horites in their hill country of Seir as far as El-paran on the border of the wilderness. ⁷ Then they turned back and came to En-mishpat (that is, Kadesh) and defeated all the country of the Amalekites, and also the Amorites who were dwelling in Hazazon-tamar.

⁸ Then the king of Sodom, the king of Gomorrah, the king of Admah, the king of Zeboiim, and the king of Bela (that is, Zoar) went out, and they joined battle in the Valley of Siddim ⁹ with Chedorlaomer king of Elam, Tidal king of Goiim, Amraphel king of Shinar, and Arioch king of Ellasar, four kings against five. ¹⁰ Now the Valley of Siddim was full of bitumen pits, and as the kings of Sodom and Gomorrah fled, some fell into them, and the rest fled to the hill country. ¹¹ So the enemy took all the possessions of Sodom and Gomorrah, and all their provisions, and went their way. ¹² They also took Lot, the son of Abram's brother, who was dwelling in Sodom, and his possessions, and went their way.

¹³ Then one who had escaped came and told Abram the Hebrew, who was living by the oaks of Mamre the Amorite, brother of Eshcol and of Aner. These were allies of Abram. ¹⁴ When Abram heard that his kinsman had been taken captive, he led forth his trained men, born in his house, 318 of them, and went in pursuit as far as Dan. ¹⁵ And he divided his forces against them by night,

he and his servants, and defeated them and pursued them to Hobah, north of Damascus. [16] Then he brought back all the possessions, and also brought back his kinsman Lot with his possessions, and the women and the people.

[17] After his return from the defeat of Chedorlaomer and the kings who were with him, the king of Sodom went out to meet him at the Valley of Shaveh (that is, the King's Valley). [18] And Melchizedek king of Salem brought out bread and wine. (He was priest of God Most High.) [19] And he blessed him and said,

"Blessed be Abram by God Most High,
    Possessor of heaven and earth;
[20] and blessed be God Most High,
    who has delivered your enemies into your hand!"

And Abram gave him a tenth of everything. [21] And the king of Sodom said to Abram, "Give me the persons, but take the goods for yourself." [22] But Abram said to the king of Sodom, "I have lifted my hand to the LORD, God Most High, Possessor of heaven and earth, [23] that I would not take a thread or a sandal strap or anything that is yours, lest you should say, 'I have made Abram rich.' [24] I will take nothing but what the young men have eaten, and the share of the men who went with me. Let Aner, Eshcol, and Mamre take their share."

OBSERVE: WHAT DOES THE PASSAGE SAY?

Step 1: Setting and Summary

Key Characters and Locations

CHARACTERS: LOCATIONS:

Summary of the Passage

What Stood Out to You or Piqued Your Curiosity?

Step 2: Key Words and Phrases

NOTES

INTERPRET: WHAT DOES THE PASSAGE MEAN?

Step 3: What Was Hard to Understand?

Questions

Insights from Cross-References, Other Translations, and the Context

Step 4: What Did You Learn about God?

Refer to the attributes of God in Tool 4 if needed.

NOTES

APPLY: HOW WILL YOU APPLY THE PASSAGE?

Step 5: What Did You Learn about People?

Others

Yourself

Wrap Up: What Did You Discover in the Scriptures That Was Important to You?

3

GOD'S COVENANT WITH ABRAM

Genesis 15:1-21

GOD'S COVENANT WITH ABRAM
Genesis 15:1–21

¹After these things the word of the LORD came to Abram in a vision: "Fear not, Abram, I am your shield; your reward shall be very great." ²But Abram said, "O LORD God, what will you give me, for I continue childless, and the heir of my house is Eliezer of Damascus?" ³And Abram said, "Behold, you have given me no offspring, and a member of my household will be my heir." ⁴And behold, the word of the LORD came to him: "This man shall not be your heir; your very own son shall be your heir." ⁵And he brought him outside and said, "Look toward heaven, and number the stars, if you are able to number them." Then he said to him, "So shall your offspring be." ⁶And he believed the LORD, and he counted it to him as righteousness.

⁷And he said to him, "I am the LORD who brought you out from Ur of the Chaldeans to give you this land to possess." ⁸But he said, "O Lord GOD, how am I to know that I shall possess it?" ⁹He said to him, "Bring me a heifer three years old, a female goat three years old, a ram three years old, a turtledove, and a young pigeon." ¹⁰And he brought him all these, cut them in half, and laid each half over against the other. But he did not cut the birds in half. ¹¹And when birds of prey came down on the carcasses, Abram drove them away.

¹²As the sun was going down, a deep sleep fell on Abram. And behold, dreadful and great darkness fell upon him. ¹³Then the LORD said to Abram, "Know for certain that your offspring will be sojourners in a land that is not theirs and will be servants there, and they will be afflicted for four hundred years. ¹⁴But I will bring judgment on the nation that they serve, and afterward they shall come out with great possessions. ¹⁵As for you, you shall go to your fathers in peace; you shall be buried in a good old age. ¹⁶And they shall come back here in the fourth generation, for the iniquity of the Amorites is not yet complete."

¹⁷ When the sun had gone down and it was dark, behold, a smoking fire pot and a flaming torch passed between these pieces. ¹⁸ On that day the LORD made a covenant with Abram, saying, "To your offspring I give this land, from the river of Egypt to the great river, the river Euphrates, ¹⁹ the land of the Kenites, the Kenizzites, the Kadmonites, ²⁰ the Hittites, the Perizzites, the Rephaim, ²¹ the Amorites, the Canaanites, the Girgashites and the Jebusites."

NOTES

OBSERVE: WHAT DOES THE PASSAGE SAY?

Step 1: Setting and Summary

Key Characters and Locations

CHARACTERS:

LOCATIONS:

Summary of the Passage

What Stood Out to You or Piqued Your Curiosity?

Step 2: Key Words and Phrases

NOTES

INTERPRET: WHAT DOES THE PASSAGE MEAN?

Step 3: What Was Hard to Understand?

Questions

Insights from Cross-References, Other Translations, and the Context

Step 4: What Did You Learn about God?

Refer to the attributes of God in Tool 4 if needed.

NOTES

APPLY: HOW WILL YOU APPLY THE PASSAGE?

Step 5: What Did You Learn about People?

Others

Yourself

Wrap Up: What Did You Discover in the Scriptures That Was Important to You?

4

SARAI, HAGAR, AND THE PROMISE OF A SON

Genesis 16:1–17:27

SARAI, HAGAR, AND THE
PROMISE OF A SON
Genesis 16:1–17:27

¹ Now Sarai, Abram's wife, had borne him no children. She had a female Egyptian servant whose name was Hagar. ² And Sarai said to Abram, "Behold now, the LORD has prevented me from bearing children. Go in to my servant; it may be that I shall obtain children by her." And Abram listened to the voice of Sarai. ³ So, after Abram had lived ten years in the land of Canaan, Sarai, Abram's wife, took Hagar the Egyptian, her servant, and gave her to Abram her husband as a wife. ⁴ And he went in to Hagar, and she conceived. And when she saw that she had conceived, she looked with contempt on her mistress. ⁵ And Sarai said to Abram, "May the wrong done to me be on you! I gave my servant to your embrace, and when she saw that she had conceived, she looked on me with contempt. May the LORD judge between you and me!" ⁶ But Abram said to Sarai, "Behold, your servant is in your power; do to her as you please." Then Sarai dealt harshly with her, and she fled from her.

⁷ The angel of the LORD found her by a spring of water in the wilderness, the spring on the way to Shur. ⁸ And he said, "Hagar, servant of Sarai, where have you come from and where are you going?" She said, "I am fleeing from my mistress Sarai." ⁹ The angel of the LORD said to her, "Return to your mistress and submit to her." ¹⁰ The angel of the LORD also said to her, "I will surely multiply your offspring so that they cannot be numbered for multitude." ¹¹ And the angel of the LORD said to her,

> "Behold, you are pregnant
>   and shall bear a son.
> You shall call his name Ishmael,
>   because the LORD has listened to your affliction.

¹²　He shall be a wild donkey of a man,

> his hand against everyone
> and everyone's hand against him,
> and he shall dwell over against all his kinsmen."

¹³ So she called the name of the LORD who spoke to her, "You are a God of seeing," for she said, "Truly here I have seen him who looks after me." ¹⁴ Therefore the well was called Beer-lahai-roi; it lies between Kadesh and Bered.

¹⁵ And Hagar bore Abram a son, and Abram called the name of his son, whom Hagar bore, Ishmael. ¹⁶ Abram was eighty-six years old when Hagar bore Ishmael to Abram.

^{17:1} When Abram was ninety-nine years old the LORD appeared to Abram and said to him, "I am God Almighty; walk before me, and be blameless, ² that I may make my covenant between me and you, and may multiply you greatly." ³ Then Abram fell on his face. And God said to him, ⁴ "Behold, my covenant is with you, and you shall be the father of a multitude of nations. ⁵ No longer shall your name be called Abram, but your name shall be Abraham, for I have made you the father of a multitude of nations. ⁶ I will make you exceedingly fruitful, and I will make you into nations, and kings shall come from you. ⁷ And I will establish my covenant between me and you and your offspring after you throughout their generations for an everlasting covenant, to be God to you and to your offspring after you. ⁸ And I will give to you and to your offspring after you the land of your sojournings, all the land of Canaan, for an everlasting possession, and I will be their God."

⁹ And God said to Abraham, "As for you, you shall keep my covenant, you and your offspring after you throughout their generations. ¹⁰ This is my covenant, which you shall keep, between me and you and your offspring after you: Every male among you shall be circumcised. ¹¹ You shall be circumcised in the flesh of your foreskins, and it shall be a sign of the covenant between me

and you. [12] He who is eight days old among you shall be circumcised. Every male throughout your generations, whether born in your house or bought with your money from any foreigner who is not of your offspring, [13] both he who is born in your house and he who is bought with your money, shall surely be circumcised. So shall my covenant be in your flesh an everlasting covenant. [14] Any uncircumcised male who is not circumcised in the flesh of his foreskin shall be cut off from his people; he has broken my covenant."

[15] And God said to Abraham, "As for Sarai your wife, you shall not call her name Sarai, but Sarah shall be her name. [16] I will bless her, and moreover, I will give you a son by her. I will bless her, and she shall become nations; kings of peoples shall come from her." [17] Then Abraham fell on his face and laughed and said to himself, "Shall a child be born to a man who is a hundred years old? Shall Sarah, who is ninety years old, bear a child?" [18] And Abraham said to God, "Oh that Ishmael might live before you!" [19] God said, "No, but Sarah your wife shall bear you a son, and you shall call his name Isaac. I will establish my covenant with him as an everlasting covenant for his offspring after him. [20] As for Ishmael, I have heard you; behold, I have blessed him and will make him fruitful and multiply him greatly. He shall father twelve princes, and I will make him into a great nation. [21] But I will establish my covenant with Isaac, whom Sarah shall bear to you at this time next year."

[22] When he had finished talking with him, God went up from Abraham. [23] Then Abraham took Ishmael his son and all those born in his house or bought with his money, every male among the men of Abraham's house, and he circumcised the flesh of their foreskins that very day, as God had said to him. [24] Abraham was ninety-nine years old when he was circumcised in the flesh of his foreskin. [25] And Ishmael his son was thirteen years old when he was circumcised in the flesh of his foreskin. [26] That very day Abraham and his son Ishmael were circumcised. [27] And all the men of his house, those born in the house and those bought with money from a foreigner, were circumcised with him.

OBSERVE: WHAT DOES THE PASSAGE SAY?

Step 1: Setting and Summary

Key Characters and Locations

CHARACTERS:

LOCATIONS:

Summary of the Passage

What Stood Out to You or Piqued Your Curiosity?

Step 2: Key Words and Phrases

NOTES

INTERPRET: WHAT DOES THE PASSAGE MEAN?

Step 3: What Was Hard to Understand?

Questions

Insights from Cross-References, Other Translations, and the Context

Step 4: What Did You Learn about God?

Refer to the attributes of God in Tool 4 if needed.

NOTES

APPLY: HOW WILL YOU APPLY THE PASSAGE?

Step 5: What Did You Learn about People?

Others

Yourself

Wrap Up: What Did You Discover in the Scriptures That Was Important to You?

5

THE VISITORS AND THE FATE OF SODOM AND GOMORRAH

Genesis 18:1–19:38

THE VISITORS AND THE FATE
OF SODOM AND GOMORRAH
Genesis 18:1–19:38

¹ And the LORD appeared to him by the oaks of Mamre, as he sat at the door of his tent in the heat of the day. ² He lifted up his eyes and looked, and behold, three men were standing in front of him. When he saw them, he ran from the tent door to meet them and bowed himself to the earth ³ and said, "O Lord, if I have found favor in your sight, do not pass by your servant. ⁴ Let a little water be brought, and wash your feet, and rest yourselves under the tree, ⁵ while I bring a morsel of bread, that you may refresh yourselves, and after that you may pass on—since you have come to your servant." So they said, "Do as you have said." ⁶ And Abraham went quickly into the tent to Sarah and said, "Quick! Three seahs of fine flour! Knead it, and make cakes." ⁷ And Abraham ran to the herd and took a calf, tender and good, and gave it to a young man, who prepared it quickly. ⁸ Then he took curds and milk and the calf that he had prepared, and set it before them. And he stood by them under the tree while they ate.

⁹ They said to him, "Where is Sarah your wife?" And he said, "She is in the tent." ¹⁰ The LORD said, "I will surely return to you about this time next year, and Sarah your wife shall have a son." And Sarah was listening at the tent door behind him. ¹¹ Now Abraham and Sarah were old, advanced in years. The way of women had ceased to be with Sarah. ¹² So Sarah laughed to herself, saying, "After I am worn out, and my lord is old, shall I have pleasure?" ¹³ The LORD said to Abraham, "Why did Sarah laugh and say, 'Shall I indeed bear a child, now that I am old?' ¹⁴ Is anything too hard for the LORD? At the appointed time I will return to you, about this time next year, and Sarah shall have a son." ¹⁵ But Sarah denied it, saying, "I did not laugh," for she was afraid. He said, "No, but you did laugh."

¹⁶ Then the men set out from there, and they looked down toward Sodom. And Abraham went with them to set them on their way. ¹⁷ The LORD said, "Shall I hide from Abraham what I am about to do, ¹⁸ seeing that Abraham shall surely become a great and mighty nation, and all the nations of the earth shall be blessed in him? ¹⁹ For I have chosen him, that he may command his children and his household after him to keep the way of the LORD by doing righteousness and justice, so that the LORD may bring to Abraham what he has promised him." ²⁰ Then the LORD said, "Because the outcry against Sodom and Gomorrah is great and their sin is very grave, ²¹ I will go down to see whether they have done altogether according to the outcry that has come to me. And if not, I will know."

²² So the men turned from there and went toward Sodom, but Abraham still stood before the LORD. ²³ Then Abraham drew near and said, "Will you indeed sweep away the righteous with the wicked? ²⁴ Suppose there are fifty righteous within the city. Will you then sweep away the place and not spare it for the fifty righteous who are in it? ²⁵ Far be it from you to do such a thing, to put the righteous to death with the wicked, so that the righteous fare as the wicked! Far be that from you! Shall not the Judge of all the earth do what is just?" ²⁶ And the LORD said, "If I find at Sodom fifty righteous in the city, I will spare the whole place for their sake."

²⁷ Abraham answered and said, "Behold, I have undertaken to speak to the Lord, I who am but dust and ashes. ²⁸ Suppose five of the fifty righteous are lacking. Will you destroy the whole city for lack of five?" And he said, "I will not destroy it if I find forty-five there." ²⁹ Again he spoke to him and said, "Suppose forty are found there." He answered, "For the sake of forty I will not do it." ³⁰ Then he said, "Oh let not the Lord be angry, and I will speak. Suppose thirty are found there." He answered, "I will not do it, if I find thirty there." ³¹ He said, "Behold, I have undertaken to speak to the Lord. Suppose twenty are found there." He answered, "For the sake of twenty I will not destroy it."

³² Then he said, "Oh let not the Lord be angry, and I will speak again but this once. Suppose ten are found there." He answered, "For the sake of ten I will not destroy it." ³³ And the Lord went his way, when he had finished speaking to Abraham, and Abraham returned to his place.

¹⁹:¹ The two angels came to Sodom in the evening, and Lot was sitting in the gate of Sodom. When Lot saw them, he rose to meet them and bowed himself with his face to the earth ² and said, "My lords, please turn aside to your servant's house and spend the night and wash your feet. Then you may rise up early and go on your way." They said, "No; we will spend the night in the town square." ³ But he pressed them strongly; so they turned aside to him and entered his house. And he made them a feast and baked unleavened bread, and they ate.

⁴ But before they lay down, the men of the city, the men of Sodom, both young and old, all the people to the last man, surrounded the house. ⁵ And they called to Lot, "Where are the men who came to you tonight? Bring them out to us, that we may know them." ⁶ Lot went out to the men at the entrance, shut the door after him, ⁷ and said, "I beg you, my brothers, do not act so wickedly. ⁸ Behold, I have two daughters who have not known any man. Let me bring them out to you, and do to them as you please. Only do nothing to these men, for they have come under the shelter of my roof." ⁹ But they said, "Stand back!" And they said, "This fellow came to sojourn, and he has become the judge! Now we will deal worse with you than with them." Then they pressed hard against the man Lot, and drew near to break the door down. ¹⁰ But the men reached out their hands and brought Lot into the house with them and shut the door. ¹¹ And they struck with blindness the men who were at the entrance of the house, both small and great, so that they wore themselves out groping for the door.

¹² Then the men said to Lot, "Have you anyone else here? Sons-in-law, sons, daughters, or anyone you have in the city, bring them out of the place.

¹³ For we are about to destroy this place, because the outcry against its people has become great before the LORD, and the LORD has sent us to destroy it." ¹⁴ So Lot went out and said to his sons-in-law, who were to marry his daughters, "Up! Get out of this place, for the LORD is about to destroy the city." But he seemed to his sons-in-law to be jesting.

¹⁵ As morning dawned, the angels urged Lot, saying, "Up! Take your wife and your two daughters who are here, lest you be swept away in the punishment of the city." ¹⁶ But he lingered. So the men seized him and his wife and his two daughters by the hand, the LORD being merciful to him, and they brought him out and set him outside the city. ¹⁷ And as they brought them out, one said, "Escape for your life. Do not look back or stop anywhere in the valley. Escape to the hills, lest you be swept away." ¹⁸ And Lot said to them, "Oh, no, my lords. ¹⁹ Behold, your servant has found favor in your sight, and you have shown me great kindness in saving my life. But I cannot escape to the hills, lest the disaster overtake me and I die. ²⁰ Behold, this city is near enough to flee to, and it is a little one. Let me escape there—is it not a little one?—and my life will be saved!" ²¹ He said to him, "Behold, I grant you this favor also, that I will not overthrow the city of which you have spoken. ²² Escape there quickly, for I can do nothing till you arrive there." Therefore the name of the city was called Zoar.

²³ The sun had risen on the earth when Lot came to Zoar. ²⁴ Then the LORD rained on Sodom and Gomorrah sulfur and fire from the LORD out of heaven. ²⁵ And he overthrew those cities, and all the valley, and all the inhabitants of the cities, and what grew on the ground. ²⁶ But Lot's wife, behind him, looked back, and she became a pillar of salt.

²⁷ And Abraham went early in the morning to the place where he had stood before the LORD. ²⁸ And he looked down toward Sodom and Gomorrah and toward all the land of the valley, and he looked and, behold, the smoke of the land went up like the smoke of a furnace.

²⁹ So it was that, when God destroyed the cities of the valley, God remembered Abraham and sent Lot out of the midst of the overthrow when he overthrew the cities in which Lot had lived.

³⁰ Now Lot went up out of Zoar and lived in the hills with his two daughters, for he was afraid to live in Zoar. So he lived in a cave with his two daughters. ³¹ And the firstborn said to the younger, "Our father is old, and there is not a man on earth to come in to us after the manner of all the earth. ³² Come, let us make our father drink wine, and we will lie with him, that we may preserve offspring from our father." ³³ So they made their father drink wine that night. And the firstborn went in and lay with her father. He did not know when she lay down or when she arose.

³⁴ The next day, the firstborn said to the younger, "Behold, I lay last night with my father. Let us make him drink wine tonight also. Then you go in and lie with him, that we may preserve offspring from our father." ³⁵ So they made their father drink wine that night also. And the younger arose and lay with him, and he did not know when she lay down or when she arose. ³⁶ Thus both the daughters of Lot became pregnant by their father. ³⁷ The firstborn bore a son and called his name Moab. He is the father of the Moabites to this day. ³⁸ The younger also bore a son and called his name Ben-ammi. He is the father of the Ammonites to this day.

OBSERVE: WHAT DOES THE PASSAGE SAY?

Step 1: Setting and Summary

Key Characters and Locations

CHARACTERS:

LOCATIONS:

Summary of the Passage

What Stood Out to You or Piqued Your Curiosity?

Step 2: Key Words and Phrases

NOTES

INTERPRET: WHAT DOES THE PASSAGE MEAN?

Step 3: What Was Hard to Understand?

Questions

Insights from Cross-References, Other Translations, and the Context

Step 4: What Did You Learn about God?

Refer to the attributes of God in Tool 4 if needed.

NOTES

APPLY: HOW WILL YOU APPLY THE PASSAGE?

Step 5: What Did You Learn about People?

Others

Yourself

Wrap Up: What Did You Discover in the Scriptures That Was Important to You?

6

ABRAHAM AND ABIMELECH, ISAAC AND ISHMAEL

Genesis 20:1–21:34

ABRAHAM AND ABIMELECH, ISAAC AND ISHMAEL
Genesis 20:1–21:34

¹ From there Abraham journeyed toward the territory of the Negeb and lived between Kadesh and Shur; and he sojourned in Gerar. ² And Abraham said of Sarah his wife, "She is my sister." And Abimelech king of Gerar sent and took Sarah. ³ But God came to Abimelech in a dream by night and said to him, "Behold, you are a dead man because of the woman whom you have taken, for she is a man's wife." ⁴ Now Abimelech had not approached her. So he said, "Lord, will you kill an innocent people? ⁵ Did he not himself say to me, 'She is my sister'? And she herself said, 'He is my brother.' In the integrity of my heart and the innocence of my hands I have done this." ⁶ Then God said to him in the dream, "Yes, I know that you have done this in the integrity of your heart, and it was I who kept you from sinning against me. Therefore I did not let you touch her. ⁷ Now then, return the man's wife, for he is a prophet, so that he will pray for you, and you shall live. But if you do not return her, know that you shall surely die, you and all who are yours."

⁸ So Abimelech rose early in the morning and called all his servants and told them all these things. And the men were very much afraid. ⁹ Then Abimelech called Abraham and said to him, "What have you done to us? And how have I sinned against you, that you have brought on me and my kingdom a great sin? You have done to me things that ought not to be done." ¹⁰ And Abimelech said to Abraham, "What did you see, that you did this thing?" ¹¹ Abraham said, "I did it because I thought, 'There is no fear of God at all in this place, and they will kill me because of my wife.' ¹² Besides, she is indeed my sister, the daughter of my father though not the daughter of my mother, and she became my wife. ¹³ And when God caused me to wander from my

father's house, I said to her, 'This is the kindness you must do me: at every place to which we come, say of me, "He is my brother."'"

¹⁴ Then Abimelech took sheep and oxen, and male servants and female servants, and gave them to Abraham, and returned Sarah his wife to him. ¹⁵ And Abimelech said, "Behold, my land is before you; dwell where it pleases you." ¹⁶ To Sarah he said, "Behold, I have given your brother a thousand pieces of silver. It is a sign of your innocence in the eyes of all who are with you, and before everyone you are vindicated." ¹⁷ Then Abraham prayed to God, and God healed Abimelech, and also healed his wife and female slaves so that they bore children. ¹⁸ For the LORD had closed all the wombs of the house of Abimelech because of Sarah, Abraham's wife.

²¹:¹ The LORD visited Sarah as he had said, and the LORD did to Sarah as he had promised. ² And Sarah conceived and bore Abraham a son in his old age at the time of which God had spoken to him. ³ Abraham called the name of his son who was born to him, whom Sarah bore him, Isaac. ⁴ And Abraham circumcised his son Isaac when he was eight days old, as God had commanded him. ⁵ Abraham was a hundred years old when his son Isaac was born to him. ⁶ And Sarah said, "God has made laughter for me; everyone who hears will laugh over me." ⁷ And she said, "Who would have said to Abraham that Sarah would nurse children? Yet I have borne him a son in his old age."

⁸ And the child grew and was weaned. And Abraham made a great feast on the day that Isaac was weaned. ⁹ But Sarah saw the son of Hagar the Egyptian, whom she had borne to Abraham, laughing. ¹⁰ So she said to Abraham, "Cast out this slave woman with her son, for the son of this slave woman shall not be heir with my son Isaac." ¹¹ And the thing was very displeasing to Abraham on account of his son. ¹² But God said to Abraham, "Be not displeased because of the boy and because of your slave woman. Whatever Sarah says to you, do as she tells you, for through Isaac shall your offspring be named. ¹³ And I will make a nation of the son of the slave woman also, because he

is your offspring." ¹⁴ So Abraham rose early in the morning and took bread and a skin of water and gave it to Hagar, putting it on her shoulder, along with the child, and sent her away. And she departed and wandered in the wilderness of Beersheba.

¹⁵ When the water in the skin was gone, she put the child under one of the bushes. ¹⁶ Then she went and sat down opposite him a good way off, about the distance of a bowshot, for she said, "Let me not look on the death of the child." And as she sat opposite him, she lifted up her voice and wept. ¹⁷ And God heard the voice of the boy, and the angel of God called to Hagar from heaven and said to her, "What troubles you, Hagar? Fear not, for God has heard the voice of the boy where he is. ¹⁸ Up! Lift up the boy, and hold him fast with your hand, for I will make him into a great nation." ¹⁹ Then God opened her eyes, and she saw a well of water. And she went and filled the skin with water and gave the boy a drink. ²⁰ And God was with the boy, and he grew up. He lived in the wilderness and became an expert with the bow. ²¹ He lived in the wilderness of Paran, and his mother took a wife for him from the land of Egypt.

²² At that time Abimelech and Phicol the commander of his army said to Abraham, "God is with you in all that you do. ²³ Now therefore swear to me here by God that you will not deal falsely with me or with my descendants or with my posterity, but as I have dealt kindly with you, so you will deal with me and with the land where you have sojourned." ²⁴ And Abraham said, "I will swear."

²⁵ When Abraham reproved Abimelech about a well of water that Abimelech's servants had seized, ²⁶ Abimelech said, "I do not know who has done this thing; you did not tell me, and I have not heard of it until today." ²⁷ So Abraham took sheep and oxen and gave them to Abimelech, and the two men made a covenant. ²⁸ Abraham set seven ewe lambs of the flock apart. ²⁹ And Abimelech said to Abraham, "What is the meaning of these seven ewe

lambs that you have set apart?" ³⁰ He said, "These seven ewe lambs you will take from my hand, that this may be a witness for me that I dug this well." ³¹ Therefore that place was called Beersheba, because there both of them swore an oath. ³² So they made a covenant at Beersheba. Then Abimelech and Phicol the commander of his army rose up and returned to the land of the Philistines. ³³ Abraham planted a tamarisk tree in Beersheba and called there on the name of the LORD, the Everlasting God. ³⁴ And Abraham sojourned many days in the land of the Philistines.

NOTES

OBSERVE: WHAT DOES THE PASSAGE SAY?

Step 1: Setting and Summary

Key Characters and Locations

CHARACTERS:

LOCATIONS:

Summary of the Passage

What Stood Out to You or Piqued Your Curiosity?

Step 2: Key Words and Phrases

NOTES

INTERPRET: WHAT DOES THE PASSAGE MEAN?

Step 3: What Was Hard to Understand?

Questions

Insights from Cross-References, Other Translations, and the Context

Step 4: What Did You Learn about God?

Refer to the attributes of God in Tool 4 if needed.

NOTES

APPLY: HOW WILL YOU APPLY THE PASSAGE?

Step 5: What Did You Learn about People?

Others

Yourself

Wrap Up: What Did You Discover in the Scriptures That Was Important to You?

7

ISAAC ON THE ALTAR

Genesis 22:1-24

ISAAC ON THE ALTAR
Genesis 22:1–24

[1] After these things God tested Abraham and said to him, "Abraham!" And he said, "Here I am." [2] He said, "Take your son, your only son Isaac, whom you love, and go to the land of Moriah, and offer him there as a burnt offering on one of the mountains of which I shall tell you." [3] So Abraham rose early in the morning, saddled his donkey, and took two of his young men with him, and his son Isaac. And he cut the wood for the burnt offering and arose and went to the place of which God had told him. [4] On the third day Abraham lifted up his eyes and saw the place from afar. [5] Then Abraham said to his young men, "Stay here with the donkey; I and the boy will go over there and worship and come again to you." [6] And Abraham took the wood of the burnt offering and laid it on Isaac his son. And he took in his hand the fire and the knife. So they went both of them together. [7] And Isaac said to his father Abraham, "My father!" And he said, "Here I am, my son." He said, "Behold, the fire and the wood, but where is the lamb for a burnt offering?" [8] Abraham said, "God will provide for himself the lamb for a burnt offering, my son." So they went both of them together.

[9] When they came to the place of which God had told him, Abraham built the altar there and laid the wood in order and bound Isaac his son and laid him on the altar, on top of the wood. [10] Then Abraham reached out his hand and took the knife to slaughter his son. [11] But the angel of the LORD called to him from heaven and said, "Abraham, Abraham!" And he said, "Here I am." [12] He said, "Do not lay your hand on the boy or do anything to him, for now I know that you fear God, seeing you have not withheld your son, your only son, from me." [13] And Abraham lifted up his eyes and looked, and behold, behind him was a ram, caught in a thicket by his horns. And Abraham went and took the ram and offered it up as a burnt offering instead of his son.

¹⁴ So Abraham called the name of that place, "The LORD will provide"; as it is said to this day, "On the mount of the LORD it shall be provided."

¹⁵ And the angel of the LORD called to Abraham a second time from heaven ¹⁶ and said, "By myself I have sworn, declares the LORD, because you have done this and have not withheld your son, your only son, ¹⁷ I will surely bless you, and I will surely multiply your offspring as the stars of heaven and as the sand that is on the seashore. And your offspring shall possess the gate of his enemies, ¹⁸ and in your offspring shall all the nations of the earth be blessed, because you have obeyed my voice." ¹⁹ So Abraham returned to his young men, and they arose and went together to Beersheba. And Abraham lived at Beersheba.

²⁰ Now after these things it was told to Abraham, "Behold, Milcah also has borne children to your brother Nahor: ²¹ Uz his firstborn, Buz his brother, Kemuel the father of Aram, ²² Chesed, Hazo, Pildash, Jidlaph, and Bethuel." ²³ (Bethuel fathered Rebekah.) These eight Milcah bore to Nahor, Abraham's brother. ²⁴ Moreover, his concubine, whose name was Reumah, bore Tebah, Gaham, Tahash, and Maacah.

NOTES

OBSERVE: WHAT DOES THE PASSAGE SAY?

Step 1: Setting and Summary

Key Characters and Locations

CHARACTERS:

LOCATIONS:

Summary of the Passage

What Stood Out to You or Piqued Your Curiosity?

Step 2: Key Words and Phrases

NOTES

INTERPRET: WHAT DOES THE PASSAGE MEAN?

Step 3: What Was Hard to Understand?

Questions

Insights from Cross-References, Other Translations, and the Context

Step 4: What Did You Learn about God?

Refer to the attributes of God in Tool 4 if needed.

NOTES

APPLY: HOW WILL YOU APPLY THE PASSAGE?

Step 5: What Did You Learn about People?

Others

Yourself

Wrap Up: What Did You Discover in the Scriptures That Was Important to You?

8

THE BURIAL OF SARAH
AND A BRIDE FOR ISAAC

Genesis 23:1–25:18

THE BURIAL OF SARAH AND
A BRIDE FOR ISAAC
Genesis 23:1–25:18

¹Sarah lived 127 years; these were the years of the life of Sarah. ²And Sarah died at Kiriath-arba (that is, Hebron) in the land of Canaan, and Abraham went in to mourn for Sarah and to weep for her. ³And Abraham rose up from before his dead and said to the Hittites, ⁴"I am a sojourner and foreigner among you; give me property among you for a burying place, that I may bury my dead out of my sight." ⁵The Hittites answered Abraham, ⁶"Hear us, my lord; you are a prince of God among us. Bury your dead in the choicest of our tombs. None of us will withhold from you his tomb to hinder you from burying your dead." ⁷Abraham rose and bowed to the Hittites, the people of the land. ⁸And he said to them, "If you are willing that I should bury my dead out of my sight, hear me and entreat for me Ephron the son of Zohar, ⁹that he may give me the cave of Machpelah, which he owns; it is at the end of his field. For the full price let him give it to me in your presence as property for a burying place."

¹⁰Now Ephron was sitting among the Hittites, and Ephron the Hittite answered Abraham in the hearing of the Hittites, of all who went in at the gate of his city, ¹¹"No, my lord, hear me: I give you the field, and I give you the cave that is in it. In the sight of the sons of my people I give it to you. Bury your dead." ¹²Then Abraham bowed down before the people of the land. ¹³And he said to Ephron in the hearing of the people of the land, "But if you will, hear me: I give the price of the field. Accept it from me, that I may bury my dead there." ¹⁴Ephron answered Abraham, ¹⁵"My lord, listen to me: a piece of land worth four hundred shekels of silver, what is that between you and me? Bury your dead." ¹⁶Abraham listened to Ephron, and Abraham weighed out for Ephron the silver that he had named in the hearing of the

Hittites, four hundred shekels of silver, according to the weights current among the merchants.

¹⁷ So the field of Ephron in Machpelah, which was to the east of Mamre, the field with the cave that was in it and all the trees that were in the field, throughout its whole area, was made over ¹⁸ to Abraham as a possession in the presence of the Hittites, before all who went in at the gate of his city. ¹⁹ After this, Abraham buried Sarah his wife in the cave of the field of Machpelah east of Mamre (that is, Hebron) in the land of Canaan. ²⁰ The field and the cave that is in it were made over to Abraham as property for a burying place by the Hittites.

²⁴·¹ Now Abraham was old, well advanced in years. And the LORD had blessed Abraham in all things. ² And Abraham said to his servant, the oldest of his household, who had charge of all that he had, "Put your hand under my thigh, ³ that I may make you swear by the LORD, the God of heaven and God of the earth, that you will not take a wife for my son from the daughters of the Canaanites, among whom I dwell, ⁴ but will go to my country and to my kindred, and take a wife for my son Isaac." ⁵ The servant said to him, "Perhaps the woman may not be willing to follow me to this land. Must I then take your son back to the land from which you came?" ⁶ Abraham said to him, "See to it that you do not take my son back there. ⁷ The LORD, the God of heaven, who took me from my father's house and from the land of my kindred, and who spoke to me and swore to me, 'To your offspring I will give this land,' he will send his angel before you, and you shall take a wife for my son from there. ⁸ But if the woman is not willing to follow you, then you will be free from this oath of mine; only you must not take my son back there." ⁹ So the servant put his hand under the thigh of Abraham his master and swore to him concerning this matter.

¹⁰ Then the servant took ten of his master's camels and departed, taking all sorts of choice gifts from his master; and he arose and went to Mesopotamia

to the city of Nahor. ¹¹ And he made the camels kneel down outside the city by the well of water at the time of evening, the time when women go out to draw water. ¹² And he said, "O LORD, God of my master Abraham, please grant me success today and show steadfast love to my master Abraham. ¹³ Behold, I am standing by the spring of water, and the daughters of the men of the city are coming out to draw water. ¹⁴ Let the young woman to whom I shall say, 'Please let down your jar that I may drink,' and who shall say, 'Drink, and I will water your camels'—let her be the one whom you have appointed for your servant Isaac. By this I shall know that you have shown steadfast love to my master."

¹⁵ Before he had finished speaking, behold, Rebekah, who was born to Bethuel the son of Milcah, the wife of Nahor, Abraham's brother, came out with her water jar on her shoulder. ¹⁶ The young woman was very attractive in appearance, a maiden whom no man had known. She went down to the spring and filled her jar and came up. ¹⁷ Then the servant ran to meet her and said, "Please give me a little water to drink from your jar." ¹⁸ She said, "Drink, my lord." And she quickly let down her jar upon her hand and gave him a drink. ¹⁹ When she had finished giving him a drink, she said, "I will draw water for your camels also, until they have finished drinking." ²⁰ So she quickly emptied her jar into the trough and ran again to the well to draw water, and she drew for all his camels. ²¹ The man gazed at her in silence to learn whether the LORD had prospered his journey or not.

²² When the camels had finished drinking, the man took a gold ring weighing a half shekel, and two bracelets for her arms weighing ten gold shekels, ²³ and said, "Please tell me whose daughter you are. Is there room in your father's house for us to spend the night?" ²⁴ She said to him, "I am the daughter of Bethuel the son of Milcah, whom she bore to Nahor." ²⁵ She added, "We have plenty of both straw and fodder, and room to spend the night." ²⁶ The man bowed his head and worshiped the LORD ²⁷ and said, "Blessed be the

LORD, the God of my master Abraham, who has not forsaken his steadfast love and his faithfulness toward my master. As for me, the LORD has led me in the way to the house of my master's kinsmen." ²⁸ Then the young woman ran and told her mother's household about these things.

²⁹ Rebekah had a brother whose name was Laban. Laban ran out toward the man, to the spring. ³⁰ As soon as he saw the ring and the bracelets on his sister's arms, and heard the words of Rebekah his sister, "Thus the man spoke to me," he went to the man. And behold, he was standing by the camels at the spring. ³¹ He said, "Come in, O blessed of the LORD. Why do you stand outside? For I have prepared the house and a place for the camels." ³² So the man came to the house and unharnessed the camels, and gave straw and fodder to the camels, and there was water to wash his feet and the feet of the men who were with him. ³³ Then food was set before him to eat. But he said, "I will not eat until I have said what I have to say." He said, "Speak on."

³⁴ So he said, "I am Abraham's servant. ³⁵ The LORD has greatly blessed my master, and he has become great. He has given him flocks and herds, silver and gold, male servants and female servants, camels and donkeys. ³⁶ And Sarah my master's wife bore a son to my master when she was old, and to him he has given all that he has. ³⁷ My master made me swear, saying, 'You shall not take a wife for my son from the daughters of the Canaanites, in whose land I dwell, ³⁸ but you shall go to my father's house and to my clan and take a wife for my son.' ³⁹ I said to my master, 'Perhaps the woman will not follow me.' ⁴⁰ But he said to me, 'The LORD, before whom I have walked, will send his angel with you and prosper your way. You shall take a wife for my son from my clan and from my father's house. ⁴¹ Then you will be free from my oath, when you come to my clan. And if they will not give her to you, you will be free from my oath.'

⁴² "I came today to the spring and said, 'O LORD, the God of my master Abraham, if now you are prospering the way that I go, ⁴³ behold, I am standing

by the spring of water. Let the virgin who comes out to draw water, to whom I shall say, "Please give me a little water from your jar to drink," ⁴⁴ and who will say to me, "Drink, and I will draw for your camels also," let her be the woman whom the LORD has appointed for my master's son.'

⁴⁵ "Before I had finished speaking in my heart, behold, Rebekah came out with her water jar on her shoulder, and she went down to the spring and drew water. I said to her, 'Please let me drink.' ⁴⁶ She quickly let down her jar from her shoulder and said, 'Drink, and I will give your camels drink also.' So I drank, and she gave the camels drink also. ⁴⁷ Then I asked her, 'Whose daughter are you?' She said, 'The daughter of Bethuel, Nahor's son, whom Milcah bore to him.' So I put the ring on her nose and the bracelets on her arms. ⁴⁸ Then I bowed my head and worshiped the LORD and blessed the LORD, the God of my master Abraham, who had led me by the right way to take the daughter of my master's kinsman for his son. ⁴⁹ Now then, if you are going to show steadfast love and faithfulness to my master, tell me; and if not, tell me, that I may turn to the right hand or to the left."

⁵⁰ Then Laban and Bethuel answered and said, "The thing has come from the LORD; we cannot speak to you bad or good. ⁵¹ Behold, Rebekah is before you; take her and go, and let her be the wife of your master's son, as the LORD has spoken."

⁵² When Abraham's servant heard their words, he bowed himself to the earth before the LORD. ⁵³ And the servant brought out jewelry of silver and of gold, and garments, and gave them to Rebekah. He also gave to her brother and to her mother costly ornaments. ⁵⁴ And he and the men who were with him ate and drank, and they spent the night there. When they arose in the morning, he said, "Send me away to my master." ⁵⁵ Her brother and her mother said, "Let the young woman remain with us a while, at least ten days; after that she may go." ⁵⁶ But he said to them, "Do not delay me, since the LORD has prospered my way. Send me away that I may go to my master." ⁵⁷ They

said, "Let us call the young woman and ask her." ⁵⁸ And they called Rebekah and said to her, "Will you go with this man?" She said, "I will go." ⁵⁹ So they sent away Rebekah their sister and her nurse, and Abraham's servant and his men. ⁶⁰ And they blessed Rebekah and said to her,

"Our sister, may you become
    thousands of ten thousands,
and may your offspring possess
    the gate of those who hate him!"

⁶¹ Then Rebekah and her young women arose and rode on the camels and followed the man. Thus the servant took Rebekah and went his way.

⁶² Now Isaac had returned from Beer-lahai-roi and was dwelling in the Negeb. ⁶³ And Isaac went out to meditate in the field toward evening. And he lifted up his eyes and saw, and behold, there were camels coming. ⁶⁴ And Rebekah lifted up her eyes, and when she saw Isaac, she dismounted from the camel ⁶⁵ and said to the servant, "Who is that man, walking in the field to meet us?" The servant said, "It is my master." So she took her veil and covered herself. ⁶⁶ And the servant told Isaac all the things that he had done. ⁶⁷ Then Isaac brought her into the tent of Sarah his mother and took Rebekah, and she became his wife, and he loved her. So Isaac was comforted after his mother's death.

²⁵:¹ Abraham took another wife, whose name was Keturah. ² She bore him Zimran, Jokshan, Medan, Midian, Ishbak, and Shuah. ³ Jokshan fathered Sheba and Dedan. The sons of Dedan were Asshurim, Letushim, and Leummim. ⁴ The sons of Midian were Ephah, Epher, Hanoch, Abida, and Eldaah. All these were the children of Keturah. ⁵ Abraham gave all he had to Isaac. ⁶ But to the sons of his concubines Abraham gave gifts, and while he was still living he sent them away from his son Isaac, eastward to the east country.

⁷ These are the days of the years of Abraham's life, 175 years. ⁸ Abraham breathed his last and died in a good old age, an old man and full of years, and was gathered to his people. ⁹ Isaac and Ishmael his sons buried him in the cave of Machpelah, in the field of Ephron the son of Zohar the Hittite, east of Mamre, ¹⁰ the field that Abraham purchased from the Hittites. There Abraham was buried, with Sarah his wife. ¹¹ After the death of Abraham, God blessed Isaac his son. And Isaac settled at Beer-lahai-roi.

¹² These are the generations of Ishmael, Abraham's son, whom Hagar the Egyptian, Sarah's servant, bore to Abraham. ¹³ These are the names of the sons of Ishmael, named in the order of their birth: Nebaioth, the firstborn of Ishmael; and Kedar, Adbeel, Mibsam, ¹⁴ Mishma, Dumah, Massa, ¹⁵ Hadad, Tema, Jetur, Naphish, and Kedemah. ¹⁶ These are the sons of Ishmael and these are their names, by their villages and by their encampments, twelve princes according to their tribes. ¹⁷ (These are the years of the life of Ishmael: 137 years. He breathed his last and died, and was gathered to his people.) ¹⁸ They settled from Havilah to Shur, which is opposite Egypt in the direction of Assyria. He settled over against all his kinsmen.

OBSERVE: WHAT DOES THE PASSAGE SAY?

Step 1: Setting and Summary

Key Characters and Locations

CHARACTERS: LOCATIONS:

Summary of the Passage

What Stood Out to You or Piqued Your Curiosity?

Step 2: Key Words and Phrases

NOTES

INTERPRET: WHAT DOES THE PASSAGE MEAN?

Step 3: What Was Hard to Understand?

Questions

Insights from Cross-References, Other Translations, and the Context

Step 4: What Did You Learn about God?

Refer to the attributes of God in Tool 4 if needed.

NOTES

APPLY: HOW WILL YOU APPLY THE PASSAGE?

Step 5: What Did You Learn about People?

Others

Yourself

Wrap Up: What Did You Discover in the Scriptures That Was Important to You?

MEET ME IN THE BIBLE TOOL KIT

BIBLE TIMELINE

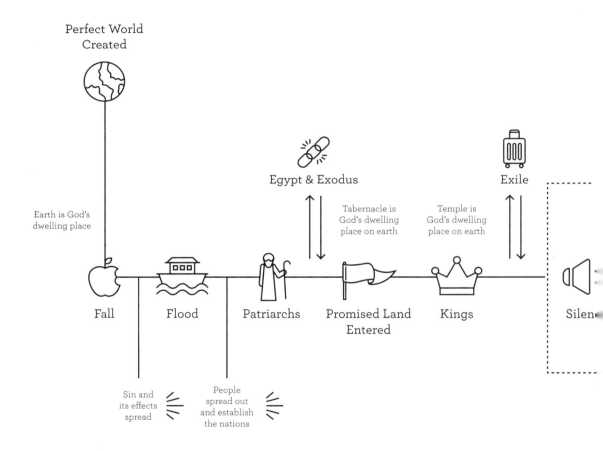

Perfect World
Created

Earth is God's
dwelling place

Egypt & Exodus

Exile

Tabernacle is
God's dwelling
place on earth

Temple is
God's dwelling
place on earth

Fall

Flood

Patriarchs

Promised Land
Entered

Kings

Silen

Sin and
its effects
spread

People
spread out
and establish
the nations

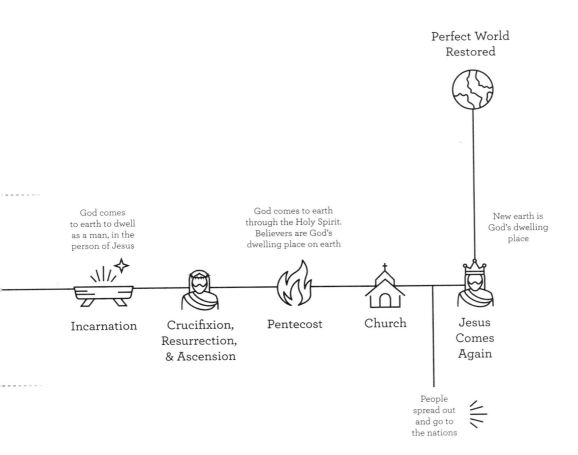

Perfect World
Restored

God comes
to earth to dwell
as a man, in the
person of Jesus

God comes to earth
through the Holy Spirit.
Believers are God's
dwelling place on earth

New earth is
God's dwelling
place

Incarnation

Crucifixion,
Resurrection,
& Ascension

Pentecost

Church

Jesus
Comes
Again

People
spread out
and go to
the nations

MAP: THE WORLD OF THE PATRIARCHS

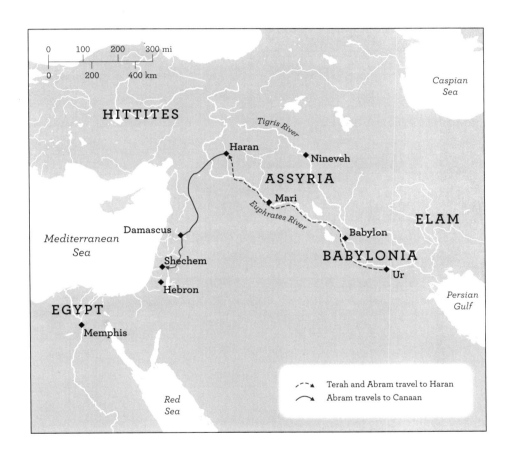

Tool 3

BIBLE GENRES

Knowing the literary style of the book of the Bible you are studying is key to correct interpretation. Just as you would approach the poems of Wordsworth differently than you would approach a history book about World War II, there are nuances to different literary styles in the Bible that must be kept in mind while interpreting and applying the Scriptures. Use this resource to identify the literary style of the book you are studying. Note that several books can be classified in more than one genre.

Genres	Books of the Bible
Apocalyptic. Visionary writings that address future judgment and salvation. Often written using symbolic language.	Daniel, Revelation
Epistle. Letters to Christians in the early church that contain doctrines of the Christian faith and instructions for Christlike living.	Romans, 1–2 Corinthians, Galatians, Ephesians, Philippians, Colossians, 1–2 Thessalonians, 1–2 Timothy, Titus, Philemon, Hebrews, James, 1–2 Peter, 1–3 John, Jude
Gospel. Historical narratives that give testimony to the genealogy, birth, life, death, resurrection, and teachings of Jesus Christ. Each Gospel is written by a different author from a different perspective and with a different emphasis.	Matthew, Mark, Luke, John

Genres	Books of the Bible
Historical Narrative. Narrations of the factual history of Israel and the early church. Historical narratives are recordings of what happened, not necessarily what should have happened had people obeyed God's commands.	Genesis, Exodus, Leviticus, Numbers, Deuteronomy, Joshua, Judges, Ruth, 1–2 Samuel, 1–2 Kings, 1–2 Chronicles, Ezra, Nehemiah, Esther, Jonah, Acts
Poetry. Expressions of joy, thanksgiving, celebration, disappointment, anxiety, and lament in poetic forms.	Psalms, Song of Solomon, Lamentations
Prophecy. God's message to his people spoken through prophets, calling God's people to repentance from sin, warning them of judgment, and revealing events yet to come.	Isaiah, Jeremiah, Ezekiel, Daniel, Hosea, Joel, Amos, Obadiah, Jonah, Micah, Nahum, Habakkuk, Zephaniah, Haggai, Zechariah, Malachi
Wisdom Literature. Writings that address life's basic questions about what it means to live faithful, God-centered lives in both big crises and everyday circumstances.	Job, some Psalms, Proverbs, Ecclesiastes

ATTRIBUTES OF GOD

Attentive. God hears and responds to the needs of his children.

Compassionate. God cares for his children and acts on their behalf.

Creator. God made everything. He is uncreated.

Deliverer. God rescues and saves his children.

Eternal. God is not limited by and exists outside of time.

Faithful. God always keeps his promises.

Generous. God gives what is best and beyond what is deserved.

Glorious. God displays his greatness and worth.

Good. God is what is best and gives what is best.

Holy. God is perfect, pure, and without sin.

Immutable/Unchanging. God never changes. He is the same yesterday, today, and tomorrow.

Incomprehensible. God is beyond our understanding. We can comprehend him in part but not in whole.

Infinite. God has no limits in his person or on his power.

Jealous. God will not share his glory with another. All glory rightfully belongs to him.

Just. God is fair in all his actions and judgments. He cannot overpunish or underpunish.

Loving. God feels and displays infinite, unconditional affection toward his children. His love for them does not depend on their worth, their response, or their merit.

Merciful. God does not give his children the punishment they deserve.

Omnipotent/Almighty. God holds all power. Nothing is too hard for God. What he wills he can accomplish.

Omnipresent. God is fully present everywhere.

Omniscient. God knows everything past, present, and future, all potential and real outcomes, all things micro and macro.

Patient/Long-Suffering. God is untiring and bears with his children.

Provider. God meets the needs of his children.

Refuge. God is a place of safety and protection for his children.

Righteous. God is always good and right.

Self-Existent. God depends on nothing and no one to give him life or existence.

Sovereign. God does everything according to his plan and pleasure. He controls all things.

Transcendant. God is not like humans. He is infinitely higher in being and action.

Truthful. Whatever God speaks or does is truth and reality.

Wise. God knows what is best and acts accordingly. He cannot choose wrongly.

Worthy. God deserves all glory and honor and praise.

Wrathful. God hates all unrighteousness.

Tool 5

BOOKMARK CONTENT

Begin by asking God to reveal himself as you read the Scriptures. Enjoy him and have fun learning and discovering!

Observe: What Does the Passage Say?

Step 1. Setting and Summary

- Read the passage, noting key characters and locations.

- Write a brief summary of the passage (about three to five sentences).

- Record what stood out to you or piqued your curiosity.

Step 2. Key Words and Phrases

- Read the passage, marking the words/phrases that are repeated or emphasized.

- Why do you think the author repeats these words? Look back at the context to help you with your answer (e.g., Who wrote it and to whom was it written?). Write down your insights.

- Are there words for which you need a better understanding (e.g., *propitiation, atonement*)? Use a dictionary or thesaurus to gain insight and note what you discover.

- Read the verses with key words/phrases in two other Bible translations. Jot down what you learn.

- Enjoy God. Talk to him and listen.

Interpret: What Does the Passage Mean?

Step 3. What Was Hard to Understand?

- Read the passage, writing down the questions that surface for you.

- Record insights you gain from the following:

  - Looking up cross-references for verses that are hard to understand.

  - Reading the passage in two other Bible translations.

  - Looking back at the context (e.g., Who wrote it and to whom was it written and when?).

Step 4. What Did You Learn about God?

- What attribute of God stood out to you in this passage?

- How does this attribute of God encourage you to anchor your hope in him? Record your discoveries.

- Enjoy God. Talk to him and listen.

Apply: How Will You Apply the Passage?

Step 5. What Did You Learn about People?

OTHERS

- What did you learn about people in this passage? How does this passage promote a love for others? Write down your thoughts.

- What did you learn that you can share with others (a friend, coworker, family member)? Pray for meaningful conversations this week.

YOURSELF

- Is there a command to obey? An example to follow? A sin to confess? A warning to heed? An encouragement to receive? Record your insights.

- What action step will you take? How will next week be different because you chose to apply what you discovered?

- Enjoy God. Talk to him and listen.

Tool 6

PRAYER PAGES

PRAYER PAGE

PRAYER PAGE

PRAYER PAGE

PRAYER PAGE

PRAYER PAGE

PRAYER PAGE

PRAYER PAGE

Tool 7

QUESTIONS FOR FURTHER THOUGHT AND DISCUSSION

These questions were written to help you think deeply about the text. Additional historical context is also given. Many questions do not have one right answer and are meant to encourage further thought and robust discussion. The bounce questions are intended to jumpstart discussion and provide an easy transition to the content.

Discussion leaders may use as many or as few questions as they'd like. The prompts on your bookmark also make good points of discussion.

Getting Started in the Story of Abraham

1. Why do you want to study the story of Abraham?

2. As you answered the context questions found in "Getting Started in the Story of Abraham," what new insight did you gain?

3. What piqued your curiosity?

4. Complete the sentence: At the end of this study, I hope to _____.

The Call of Abram and the Journey to Egypt (Genesis 11:27–13:1)

- Bounce question: Have you lived in another country? If yes, what were the biggest challenges during your transition there?

1. We learn a little about Abram's upbringing in the cross-reference Joshua 24:2. Why do you think God chose Abram, calling him out of Ur?

2. In light of God's command in Genesis 12:1, should Abram have taken Terah and Lot along when he left Ur? In light of Genesis 11:30 and the customs at the time, why do you think Abram took Lot along?

3. What do you find most surprising about God's promises to Abram in Genesis 12:1–3?

4. Turn your focus to Sarai. How do you think Sarai felt about leaving her homeland and kindred to settle in Canaan? How do you think she felt about Abram's plan while in Egypt? How do you think she felt about God's intervention on her behalf (Gen. 12:17)? What do you think Abram and Sarai's journey back to Canaan was like?

5. In what way(s) did Abram demonstrate great faith in this passage? In what way(s) does Abram's life serve as a warning?

Abram, Lot, and Melchizedek (Genesis 13:2–14:24)

- Bounce question: The text includes an epic battle scene. What is your favorite battle scene in a movie? Why?

1. What incited the separation of Abram and Lot?

2. How did Abram demonstrate faith in chapter 13? What do you learn about Lot from this passage?

3. Right after Abram and Lot separated, God spoke again to Abram. In what ways do the promises given in Genesis 12:1–3 broaden in Genesis 13:14–17? Why do you think God gave more detail after the separation?

4. Two groups went to war in Genesis 14. One group was led by King Chedorlaomer and one group was made up of city-kings (including the city-kings of Sodom and Gomorrah) who had been oppressed by King Chedorlaomer. King Chedorlaomer won the war. In what way(s) did Abram demonstrate great faith in this passage? In what way(s) do Lot's choices serve as a warning?

5. What details given about Melchizedek remind you of the Lord Jesus? Read cross-reference Hebrews 7 to gain more insight about Melchizedek.

God's Covenant with Abram (Genesis 15:1–21)

- Bounce question: How do you think our culture views binding agreements? Name a few types of agreements that are taken seriously and a few that are not.

1. Why do you think chapter 15 begins with God telling Abram not to fear? Think back to what happened in chapter 14. In what way(s) had God already demonstrated that he was Abram's shield and great reward?

2. Abram stated his angst in Genesis 15:2–3. How did God respond? What do you learn about God from his response?

3. Genesis 15:6 is a key verse in the whole story of the Bible. Read cross-reference Romans 4:1–8. What are the implications for you?

4. We read in Genesis 15 about the covenant God made with Abram. This ritual sounds strange to us, but it was the customary way to make a binding agreement at this time in history. The parties covenanting with one another would cut animals in half, tearing the flesh and spilling the blood of the animals, and then they would make the covenant in between the torn halves. The idea was to convey, "May this be done to me if I break my covenant with you." How does this add to your understanding of God's covenant with Abram?

5. Why do you think God chose to manifest his presence as a smoking fire pot and a flaming torch when the covenant was cut? Hint: Remember who wrote Genesis and for whom he was writing it. What would have been familiar about these images to the original hearers?

6. What were the requirements for Abraham and his descendants to ensure that God would keep his covenant with them?

Sarai, Hagar, and the Promise of a Son (Genesis 16:1–17:27)

- Bounce question: Do you know the meaning of your name? Have you wished to have a different name? If yes, what name would you choose?

1. Why do you think God waited so long to give Abram and Sarai a son?

2. Did Hagar have a choice in this situation? How do you think she felt? What is similar between her situation and Sarai's situation in Genesis 12:10–20?

3. When did Hagar join Abram's family? Look back at Genesis 12:15–16 for insight. In what ways was Abram's decision to go to Egypt still affecting Sarai? Hagar?

4. How do the promises given in Genesis 12:1–3 broaden in Genesis 17:4–8?

5. God chose circumcision to be the mark of the Abrahamic covenant. In the ritual cutting of circumcision, flesh is torn and blood is spilled. How does the mark of the covenant remind you of God cutting the covenant in Genesis 15? In what way(s) does the mark of the covenant point forward to the Lord Jesus, who fulfilled the Abrahamic covenant?

6. In what way(s) does God demonstrate his faithfulness in chapters 16 and 17 to Abram? To Sarai? To Hagar? To Ishmael?

The Visitors and the Fate of Sodom and Gomorrah (Genesis 18:1–19:38)

- Bounce question: Have you been invited into a discussion that impacted a lot of people? How did you feel?

1. Why did God reveal his plans to Abraham, then engage Abraham in a discussion about them? Can you think of other people in the Bible with whom God shared his plans? What do you think God was revealing about himself?

2. Did God change his mind? Use other Scripture to support your answer.

3. At this time in history, salt was used as a preservative. How does this add to your understanding of the fate of Lot's wife (Gen. 19:26)? Why do you think she looked back at Sodom?

4. What do you learn about God through his dealing with Lot? Look up Genesis 19:29 for insight.

5. Lot's daughters gave rise to the Moabites and Ammonites, both known for their conflict with the Hebrew people. In light of Lot's story and God's command in Genesis 12:1, should Abram have taken Lot along when he left Ur? How does Lot's life serve as a warning?

Abraham and Abimelech, Isaac and Ishmael (Genesis 20:1–21:34)

- Bounce question: Like Abraham, we are often tempted to tell half-truths to self-protect. What is the silliest lie you told as a child to stay out of trouble?

1. Compare the situation in Gerar to the situation in Egypt described in Genesis 12:10–20. What is similar? At this time in history, women and men were not treated as equals in value and dignity. What do we learn about how God views women through both scenarios?

2. In what way(s) did Abimelech behave more respectably than Abraham? How can we apply this story to our behavior among unbelievers?

3. Why do you think the Holy Spirit inspired the author of Genesis to record the failures of Abraham?

4. What do you think is different between Sarah's laughter in Genesis 21:6 and Ishmael's laughter in 21:9? Look up Genesis 21:9 in another Bible translation for insight.

5. After reading Genesis 21, try to put yourself in the place of others in this account. How do you think Abraham felt about casting Ishmael out? How do you think this felt to Ishmael? To Hagar? What evidence do you see in the passage that God continued to look after Hagar and Ishmael?

6. What can we learn from the dealings between Abraham and Abimelech, men of different beliefs and different territories?

7. Genesis 21 ends with Abraham owning a well in Canaan, where he planted a tree. Thinking back to God's promises given to Abraham, why are these seemingly small things significant?

Isaac on the Altar (Genesis 22:1–24)

- Bounce question: Human nature is often slow to obey, particularly when obedience means doing something we don't want to do. When you were a kid, what rule were you regularly tempted to disregard? Why?

1. Look back at the following verses in Genesis: 17:23; 21:14; and 22:3. What pattern do you observe in Abraham? Is there an area of your life in which to apply his example?

2. How many descendants did Abraham have at this time? Try to imagine being in Abraham's place. How would you have felt about this command from God? What questions would you have?

3. Why do you think God chose to test Abraham in this way?

4. Consider Isaac's actions in chapter 22. What do you learn about his character?

5. In what way(s) does Abraham image God the Father in Genesis 22? In what way(s) does Isaac image God the Son?

The Burial of Sarah and a Bride for Isaac (Genesis 23:1–25:18)

- Bounce Question: Have you ever experienced an immediate answer to prayer?

1. The focus of Genesis 23 is Abraham's purchase of a field and a place to bury Sarah. Why is it significant that Sarah is buried in this location? Hint: it was customary to be buried with one's ancestors, and her ancestors were in Mesopotamia.

2. Why is the story of Isaac getting a bride so important?

3. Consider the prayer of Abraham's servant in Genesis 24:12–14. What stands out to you about his prayer? How might your prayers model his?

4. What can you learn from Rebekah, through the way she served the servant in verses 18–21 and through her response in verses 55–59?

5. God had promised Abraham offspring, land, and blessing. Were these promises fulfilled? Be specific. Were they fulfilled to the extent Abraham expected? Were they fulfilled within his lifetime?

6. Were you surprised by Genesis 25? If so, how?

7. What have you discovered through the story of Abraham that you hope to never forget?

NOTES

1. My favorite tool is *Merriam-Webster's Collegiate Dictionary*, 11th ed. (Springfield, MA: Merriam-Webster, 2003), continually updated at https://www.merriam-webster.com.
2. I demonstrate how to use Bible Gateway (https://www.biblegateway.com/) to cross-reference in my introductory video: https://www.colleensearcy.com/.
3. Bible Gateway (https://www.biblegateway.com/) also includes footnotes.
4. I've found Tim Challies's article helpful: "Best Commentaries on Each Book of the Bible" Challies website, accessed April 29, 2024, https://challies.com/.
5. Questions 1–4 are informed by Jen Wilkin, *Women of the Word: How to Study the Bible with Both Our Hearts and Our Minds* (Wheaton, IL: Crossway, 2014).
6. For further study on Bible genres, a helpful resource is Gordon D. Fee and Douglas Stuart, *How to Read the Bible for All Its Worth* (Grand Rapids, MI: Zondervan, 2014).
7. *Merriam-Webster*, s.v. "bless," accessed May 1, 2024, https://www.merriam-webster.com/.

Also Available from the Meet Me in the Bible Series

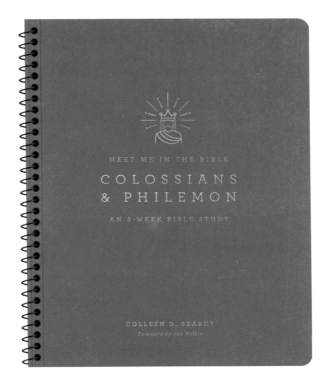

This inductive study uses a practical 5-step framework to observe and interpret Colossians and Philemon and apply it to everyday life. The Meet Me in the Bible series is a unique combination of Scripture journal and Bible reading guide.

For more information, visit **crossway.org**.